CONTENTS

Clockwork
by Philip Pullman

CREDITS

Published by Scholastic Ltd,
Villiers House,
Clarendon Avenue,
Leamington Spa,
Warwickshire CV32 5PR
Text © Angel Scott
© 1999 Scholastic Ltd
  2 3 4 5 6 7 8 9 0   9 0 1 2 3 4 5 6 7 8

Author Angel Scott
Editor Joel Lane
Assistant editor Clare Miller
Series designer Lynne Joesbury
Designer Sarah Rock
Illustrations Peter Bailey
Cover illustration Peter Bailey

Designed using Adobe Pagemaker

British Library Cataloguing-in-Publication Data
A catalogue record for this book is available
from the British Library.

ISBN 0-590-53862-4

ACKNOWLEDGEMENTS

Extracts from *Clockwork* by Philip Pullman,
illustrated by Peter Bailey
Copyright © 1996 by Philip Pullman
Illustrations copyright © 1996 by Peter Bailey
First published in Great Britain by Doubleday, a
division of Transworld Publishers Ltd

INTRODUCTION

Clockwork
by Philip Pullman

WHAT IS THE PLOT OF THE STORY?

The story is set a long time ago in a little German town. It has a complicated plot: a story within a story! Karl the apprentice clock-maker has failed to make a mechanical figure for the town's clock to end his apprenticeship. His friend, Fritz the story-teller, is telling a story which suddenly starts to come alive as the characters in the story appear. One of these characters, the mysterious Dr Kalmenius, offers to help Karl by giving him a mechanical figure for the clock. Karl accepts the offer without considering the possible consequences...

WHAT'S SO GOOD ABOUT THE BOOK?

The book is an exciting, frightening supernatural story with many elements of traditional fairy stories and horror stories in it. It is cleverly written and structured so that it is simple and exciting to read, but very complicated when you come to work it all out and understand it. The story is told in three different voices, and all the pieces overlap and interconnect. In fact, this book is like clockwork, with all the little cogs and wheels working together to create an intricate and powerful story.

ABOUT PHILIP PULLMAN

Philip Pullman used to be a teacher before he became a full-time writer. He has written many plays and novels, several of which (including *Clockwork*) have won major literary prizes. He writes in a book-lined shed at the bottom of his garden in Oxford. He thinks that writing for children should be about big themes – *love, loyalty, the place of religion and science in life, what it really means to be human* – and he does not write down to his readers. He believes that the story and its structure are the most important elements in good storytelling; and that writing is a craft which writers have to learn, using words skilfully as the tools of their trade.

READ & RESPOND
3

Cover clues

● Look carefully at the front cover of *Clockwork*. Talk about the questions below.

What can you see on the front cover?

What **kind** of book do you think this is going to be?

What do you think the story will be about?

What do you think *Winner of the Smarties Prize and the Carnegie Medal* means?

Does it refer to the author, Philip Pullman, or to the book?

Why do you think it is on the front cover?

Notice that the book has two titles. Do they both mean the same thing?

Why do you think the writer has given the story two titles?

What other clues does this give you about the story?

Cover clues (cont.)

● The back cover gives more information about *Clockwork*. Read the blurb and then talk about the questions.

What characters are in this story?

What kind of weather forms the background for the story?

> Tick, tock, tick, tock!
> Some stories are like that. Once you've wound them up, nothing will stop them...
>
> A tormented apprentice clock-maker – and a deadly knight in armour. A mechanical prince – and the sinister Dr Kalmenius, who some say is the devil... Wind up these characters, fit them into a story on a cold winter's evening, with the snow swirling down, and suddenly life and the story begin to merge in a peculiarly macabre – and unstoppable – way.
>
> Almost like clockwork...
>
> 'Exciting, scary, romantic and deliciously readable'
> THE GUARDIAN
>
> *Shortlisted for*
> THE CARNEGIE MEDAL
> *and* THE WHITBREAD CHILDREN'S BOOK AWARD
>
> Also by Philip Pullman:
> THE FIREWORK-MAKER'S DAUGHTER
> Gold Medal winner, Smarties Prize
>
> A CORGI YEARLING BOOK
> Illustrated by Peter Bailey
>
> UK £3.99   ISBN 0-440-86343-0
> 9 780440 863434 >

The blurb says that what happens is *Almost like clockwork.* What does this mean?

How else is the story compared to a clock?

What other adjectives are used to describe the story?

What other information have you found out from the back cover?

● Using what you have found out from the cover, write one sentence saying what **kind** of story you think *Clockwork* will be.

I think that *Clockwork* by Philip Pullman will be _____

_____

_____

What kind of story is it?

You are certain to have read many different stories. Each story is unique, but it may resemble other stories in particular ways. When this happens, we say that the stories belong to a story type or **genre**. You may particularly like one genre of story – for example, horror stories, science fiction or adventure stories.

You can often tell what genre a story belongs to from the characters, the setting, the plot and the themes.

● Think about some fairy stories, legends and supernatural stories you have read. What would you expect to find in these types of story? Fill in the chart. Some ideas have been provided to start you off.

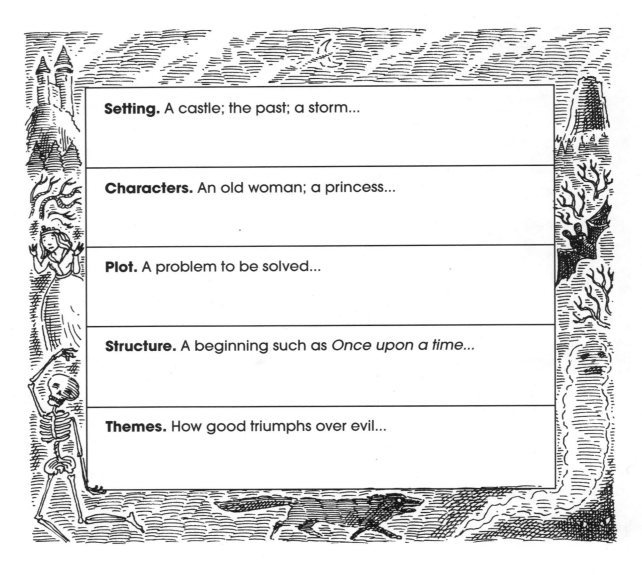

Setting. A castle; the past; a storm...

Characters. An old woman; a princess...

Plot. A problem to be solved...

Structure. A beginning such as *Once upon a time...*

Themes. How good triumphs over evil...

● Now think about *Clockwork*. Using a red pen, go through the chart again and write down what you think this story will have under each heading.

Clockwork: A Preface

A **preface** is a type of introduction. It may explain what the book is about or why it was written.

● Read 'Clockwork: A Preface' carefully. Talk about it, then fill in the spaces below.

In the old days, time was measured by _____

Nowadays, time is measured by _____

Two examples of how clockwork can be dangerous are:

1. _____

2. _____

'Tick, tock, tick, tock! Bit by bit they move, and tick us steadily on towards the grave.'

By this, I think Philip Pullman means that _____

_____

Philip Pullman compares a story to a clock by saying that _____

_____

I think Philip Pullman wrote the Preface in order to _____

_____

_____

Setting the scene

● Read the opening of Part One, up to the beginning of Fritz's Story. Think about the scene in the White Horse Tavern, and the people there.

● Your task now is to brief an artist who is drawing illustrations for a special edition of *Clockwork*. There will be two pictures to go with this opening section. You need to do rough sketches and write clear instructions for the artist. Think carefully about what should go in each picture. Re-read the opening section for details.

Here are are some ideas to get you started:

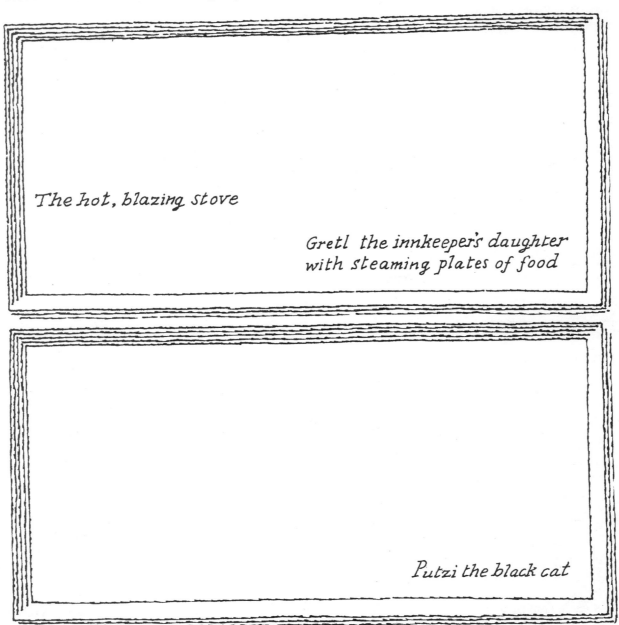

The hot, blazing stove

Gretl the innkeeper's daughter with steaming plates of food

Putzi the black cat

● Remember to help the artist by labelling each sketch.

Telling Fritz's Story

● Read Fritz's Story up to where Dr Kalmenius comes in and Fritz stops speaking.

What makes a good storyteller? **How** you tell the story is just as important as what happens. Good storytellers choose their words carefully. They vary the tone and pace, and use emphasis and expression.

● You are going to retell Fritz's story. First, you need to re-read it carefully and make notes in the box below. Bear in mind:
• You need to focus on the key events which will help to prompt you when you come to tell the story.
• You do not have to use Fritz's words. Try to make his story your own. **But** make sure that you stick to the events of Fritz's story!
• Remember: your words should create atmosphere **and** move the story along.

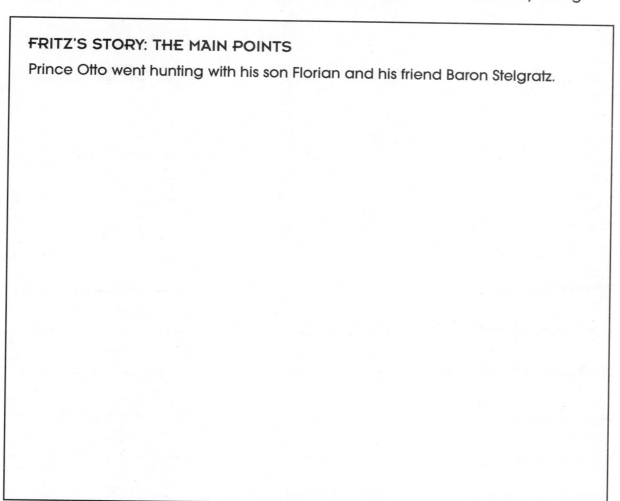

FRITZ'S STORY: THE MAIN POINTS

Prince Otto went hunting with his son Florian and his friend Baron Stelgratz.

● Now practise telling the story to a partner, using your notes to guide you. Listen to any comments that may help you improve your storytelling. When you are ready, tell the story to a group of friends or the whole class.

Dr Kalmenius

● Read on to the end of Part One.

● Annotate the picture of Dr Kalmenius with **all** the information that you have gathered about him.

Loose hood like a monk's

Skilful hands for working with fine metals

Why are the townspeople so frightened of Dr Kalmenius? _____

_____

What kind of person do you think he is? _____

_____

_____

What do you think is going to happen to Gretl? _____

_____

_____

The story of Prince Florian

Part Two is almost a separate story. It tells us more about the events described in Fritz's Story.

● Read Part Two and make some notes to answer these questions:

Part Two
Who is in the story?
Where does it take place?
What happens?
How does it end?

● Think back to Fritz's story. Can you remember:

Fritz's story
Who is in the story?
Where does it take place?
What happens?
How does it end?

● Look back to check your answers if you are not sure.

● Are the two stories the same? Or are they different? Use your notes to help you decide. Make lists in the box below:

Things that are the same	Things that are different

● Before you read Part Three, think about:
• What place has Prince Florian arrived at?
• Do you recognize his song?
• Can you guess what is about to happen now?
Read on to find out!

Gretl – and Karl

● Read on to the bottom of page 83. The story rushes towards an exciting climax. Gretl and Karl have important roles to play.

● Chart Gretl's actions as she tries to save Prince Florian and bring the story to a happy end.

TICK

        TICK

   TICK

      TICK

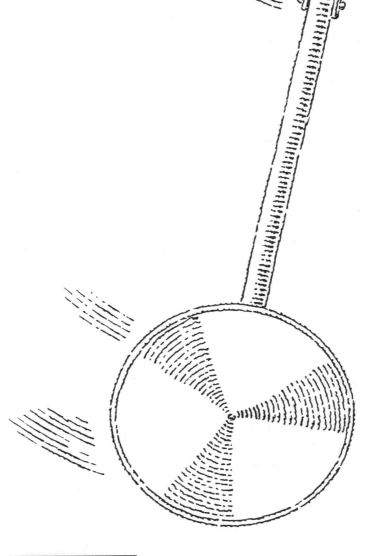

Karl – and Gretl

● Now chart Karl's course of action during Part Three of the story.

TOCK

TOCK

TOCK

TOCK

● Now see whether you can draw lines to link Gretl's actions and Karl's actions together. You will need to re-read Part Three very carefully. Notice how their actions are put together in the story. Look out for phrases like 'meanwhile' and 'at the same time' to help you see when the action moves from one character to the other.

The clock strikes ten!

● Read on to the end of *Clockwork*.

As the clock strikes ten, all the townspeople gather to see the new figure. This is a very **dramatic moment** in the story.

● You are going to act out this moment, in the following way:

1. First, ten of you need to be clockwork figures in the town clock. You could choose a figure mentioned in Part One or Part Three, or make up one of your own. Work with a partner to make a pair of figures if you like.
2. To complete the clock, two of you need to be Gretl and Prince Florian.
3. Practise your clockwork movements. Then take up your positions in the clock.
4. As your teacher reads, listen carefully for the words *The hour began to strike*. Then mime your clockwork actions, in turn, as each hour is struck.
5. When the clock finally strikes ten, all of you except Gretl and Prince Florian should become the townspeople, gathering and looking up to see the two figures waking up on the ledge high above. Improvise different reactions in the crowd. One of you could be the Burgomaster; one could be Herr Ringelmann; and Fritz's landlady might also be there. What do they see? What do they say?

● Now write about being part of the crowd in that town square. Use the back of this sheet. Describe what it felt like, what you saw and what was said.
    If you wish, use this to start you off:

> 'People were crammed shoulder to shoulder, and every face was turned up like a flower to the sun. The hour began to strike...'

'Nothing to worry about,' he said. 'It's a condition known as inflammatory oxidosis...'

You won't find the word 'oxidosis' in a dictionary. Luckily, Philip Pullman tells us what the doctor means:

> That's a typical Doctor's answer. He makes up a medical-sounding name (all <u>oxidosis</u> means is <u>rusty disease</u>) and prescribes some medicine that at least won't do any harm. That's one of the first things they teach them in medical school – or it used to be.

If he hadn't told us, could we work it out? Well, the word 'oxidise' means 'become rusty'. And the **suffix** '-osis' means something accumulating in the body and causing disease. All that the doctor has done is to make up a word that describes what he can see is wrong – in Latin!

● Two more medical-sounding suffixes are **'-itis'** and **'-phobia'**. The suffix '-itis' means 'inflammation'. The suffix '-phobia' means 'fear or dislike'. Write down some examples of words ending in '-itis' or '-phobia', and what they mean.

● Can you find any more suffixes? Use a dictionary to help.

● Try inventing some new medical conditions using these suffixes. For example, Fritz's fear of ending his story might be called 'narrative phobia' or 'narraphobia'.

Language investigation: punctuation

An interviewer once asked Philip Pullman, 'What advice would you give to aspiring writers?' This was his reply:

> Take an interest in the craft. Learn to punctuate. Buy several dictionaries and use them. If you're not sure about a point of grammar, look it up. Take a pride in the tools. Keep them sharp and bright and well-oiled. No-one else is going to look after the language if you don't.

Because he likes using long, complex sentences in his stories, Philip Pullman needs to use a lot of different punctuation marks.

● Look closely at the two opening paragraphs of Part One:

Once upon a time (when time ran by clockwork), a strange event took place in a little German town. Actually, it was a series of events, all fitting together like the parts of a clock, and although each person saw a different part, no-one saw the whole of it; but here it is, as well as I can tell it.

It began on a winter's evening, when the townsfolk were gathering in the White Horse Tavern. The snow was blowing down from the mountains, and the wind was making the bells shift restlessly in the church tower. The windows were steamed up, the stove was blazing brightly, Putzi the old black cat was snoozing on the hearth; and the air was full of the rich smells of sausage and sauerkraut, of tobacco and beer. Gretl the little barmaid, the landlord's daughter, was hurrying to and fro with foaming mugs and steaming plates.

● Mark all the punctuation in these paragraphs with a highlighter pen.

Language investigation: punctuation (cont.)

● Working with a partner, make a list of all the different punctuation marks you have highlighted. Try to work out why Philip Pullman has used each mark in the way that he has; then try to write a **rule** for each one.

For example, a capital letter is used for the name of a place or a person (White Horse Tavern, Gretl and so on). So one rule might be: **Proper names always start with a capital letter.**

If you get stuck, ask another pair or your teacher, or use a reference book.

punctuation mark	used because	rule

● Skim through *Clockwork* and find some other passages where Philip Pullman uses long, complex sentences. Some good places to look at are where:
• Dr Kalmenius makes Prince Florian (early in Part 2);
• Gretl climbs the clock tower (middle of Part 3);
• the clock strikes ten (end of Part 3).

Look carefully at the various punctuation marks used. Are they always used for the same reasons?

● Try reading the opening paragraphs without punctuation, or use a word processor to retype them without any punctuation. What happens to the meaning? Does the passage still make sense?

● Look back to what Philip Pullman said about punctuation. Do you agree with him? Why do **you** think punctuation is important?

Finishing Fritz's Story

THIS IS FRITZ: USELESS, YOU SEE. QUITE IRRESPONSIBLE. BUT THEN FRITZ WAS ONLY PLAYING AT BEING A STORYTELLER. IF HE WAS A PROPER CRAFTSMAN LIKE A CLOCKWORK-MAKER HE'D HAVE KNOWN THAT ALL ACTIONS HAVE THEIR CONSEQUENCES. FOR EVERY TICK THERE IS A TOCK. FOR EVERY ONCE UPON A TIME THERE MUST BE A STORY TO FOLLOW, BECAUSE IF A STORY DOESN'T, SOMETHING ELSE WILL, AND IT MIGHT NOT BE AS HARMLESS AS A STORY.

Fritz's story ends in mid-sentence. Gretl discovers this when she finds the crumpled up last page:

He was very tall and thin, with a prominent nose and jaw. His eyes blazed like coals in caverns of darkness. His hair was long and grey, and he wore a black cloak with a loose hood like that of a monk; he had a harsh grating voice and his expression was full of savage curiosity. And that was the man who —

● Now that you have read *Clockwork*, can you complete Fritz's Story? Remind yourself of what happens in it. Plan what happens next, and how it will end:

FRITZ'S STORY PLAN: THE ENDING

● Use your plan to write the story in rough form on a word processor. Working on screen, redraft and polish your writing until it is as good as you can make it. Then print your final version.

Word pictures

A good storyteller can describe scenes, characters and events so well that the reader or listener conjures up a vivid picture. The writer uses descriptive words and phrases to create detailed **word pictures** that are full of atmosphere.

● Re-read some of Philip Pullman's descriptions in *Clockwork*. Notice how he creates **word pictures** by giving details about each scene. You might look at:
- the opening paragraphs;
- Dr Kalmenius's arrival at the inn;
- the creation of Prince Florian;
- Gretl's journey up the clock-tower to find Florian;
- the final scene, when all the townspeople gather to see the new clock figure.

● Now you try! You are going to write a word picture, building up details to create atmosphere just like Philip Pullman.

The scene you are going to describe is: *Meanwhile, Karl had been preparing the place in the mechanism of the great clock that was set aside for his masterpiece.* We are not told anything more – it's up to you to decide on the details. Think about:
- sounds;
- sights;
- smells;

and create an atmosphere with your words.

Mystery, puzzle or wish

Clockwork is a strange and scary story. It contains many mysteries, puzzles and wishes which link together in the plot.

● Draw a line to link each character with a mystery, puzzle or wish. Think carefully! Then write a sentence explaining the nature of each link.

'I want a figure for the clock!'

_____

'I wish I had a child as sound as a bell and as true as a clock.'

_____

'If I come up with something good, the devil can have my soul!'

_____

'Find him a heart, and he will live... The heart that is given must also be kept.'

_____

'He would spend hours sitting in graveyards, contemplating the mysteries of life and death.'

_____

'I feel I'm supposed to do something, but I don't know what it is!'

_____

'His mechanism is so delicate, so perfectly balanced, that one word and one word alone will start him moving.'

_____

'Well, my friends, it's just a mystery, and I don't suppose we'll ever get to the bottom of it.'

_____

Karl

Princess Mariposa

Fritz

Gretl

Sir Ironsoul

Florian

Herr Ringelmann

Dr Kalmenius

Solving the mystery

At the end, Herr Ringelmann says about the metal knight:

> Well, my friends, it's just a mystery, and I don't suppose we'll ever get to the bottom of it.

As readers, we probably feel a bit like that about the whole book. It is a very intriguing tale.

● With a partner, talk about these questions and see whether you can come to some conclusions. After talking through each problem, write down what you think.

• Who was Dr Kalmenius? Was he *only a character in a story, after all*?

_____

_____

• Why was Fritz *the one person who might have been able to tell them the truth*?

_____

_____

• How did Gretl turn Prince Florian *from clockwork into boy*?

_____

_____

• What is this story **really** about? What is Philip Pullman trying to say to his readers?

_____

_____

_____

_____

_____

Names are important

In traditional stories, names are important. A character's name may:

- tell us something about that character;
- remind us of other stories;
- help to set the scene.

● Here are the names of some characters in *Clockwork*. Write next to each name a reason why it is suitable for that character. The first one has been done for you.

Name	Suitable because
Fritz	The story is set in Germany and this is a common German name.
Princess Mariposa	
Prince Florian	
Gretl	
Herr Ringelmann	
Dr Kalmenius	
Baron Stelgratz	
Sir Ironsoul	
Putzi	

Who tells the story?

● There are at least two storytellers (or **narrators**) in this story. Write down who is telling each part of the story:

	Narrator
Preface	
Part One	
Fritz's Story	
Part Two	
Part Three	
The boxed captions	

● Compare your list with a partner's. Discuss these questions:
• Is it confusing to have two different narrators?
• Why do you think Philip Pullman decided to write the book like that?

Do you enjoy the boxed captions (in capital letters?) They are there to do several different jobs in the book:
• some are funny asides;
• some give more information;
• some give a moral or meaning.

● Choose one caption that you particularly like. Copy it (or part of it) into the box below. Underneath the caption, explain what job it has in the book.

```



```

The Post-It Notes Master Plan

When Philip Pullman plans the shape of a story, he uses small yellow Post-It Notes. On each one, he writes a brief sentence or note, summarizing a scene. Then he gets a big piece of paper and sticks the Post-It Notes on it, moving them around to get them in the best order.

● Working in a small group, write the Post-It Notes that Philip Pullman might have used when he was planning *Clockwork*. Think back over the important scenes in the book, and imagine how Philip Pullman might have summarized each one.

You can write in the Post-It Note shapes on this page, then cut them out and move them around on a large sheet of paper until you have the same arrangement that Philip Pullman decided on. You may not need all these shapes; or you may need to draw more.

Here are two notes to get you started:

Preface clockwork and stories fate and destiny life and death	A snowy winter's night White Horse Tavern stove blazing people eating and drinking	

READ & RESPOND

'Like clockwork'

The structure of the book *Clockwork* is like a clockwork mechanism. It has interconnecting parts that move together to keep the story going. The characters move in and out of the plot, like figures in the Glockenheim Clock.

● Using your Post-It Notes Master Plan to help you, use the clock below to show the main characters and key events of the story. Show the events on the clock face, and the characters around or below the clock.

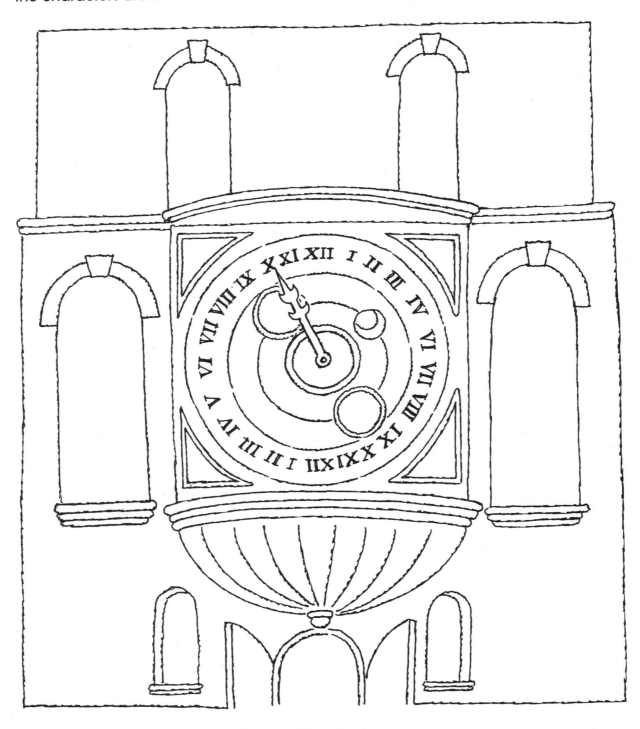

Reviewing *Clockwork*

● Read what some book reviewers have said about *Clockwork*:

'Works well... like clockwork. Clever, extremely clever.'

'A truly Gothic tale... we are in the hands of an authentic storyteller.'

'Exciting, scary, romantic and deliciously readable fairy tale which explores, with such an easy familiarity, the philosophical implications of both clockmaking and storytelling.'

'For those who might want to read spooky stories this Christmas in front of a flickering fire, this story could hardly be better.'

● Do you understand these comments? For example, what does 'Gothic' mean? And what are 'the philosophical implications of both clockmaking and storytelling'? Discuss these ideas.

● Do you agree with the quotes? If not, why not? Discuss your views.

● A magazine for children of your age wants you to write a review of *Clockwork* for its Books of the Month page. But it only has enough space for three sentences! To sum up your view of the book, you will need to think hard and choose your words carefully. Plan your review on scrap paper, then write it in the space below.

Books of the month

Clockwork by Philip Pullman   *reviewed by*

Clockwork is an exciting, scary Gothic tale with many elements of traditional stories. The story will appeal to children who love horror and the gruesome, but it also has a strong moral element. Expertly crafted, the narratives click into each other like the mechanism of a clock.

The story is set in a small German town, Glockenheim, which has a famous clock.

Part One starts on a winter night when townspeople gather in the local tavern to hear Fritz's latest ghostly story. Fritz is nervous because he has not finished the story that everyone has gathered to hear. Karl, the clockmaker's apprentice, is also there. He is due the next day to finish his apprenticeship by adding a new figure to the town's clock. Many have come for this exciting event. But Karl has not made a figure, and is deeply depressed. Fritz starts to tell his story.

Fritz's Story tells how, a few years previously, Prince Otto died tragically after a hunting trip with his son Florian. It was rumoured that when he returned to the palace with Florian, Prince Otto was no longer human but partly made of clockwork. The Royal Physician suspected that Dr Kalmenius, the master clockwork-maker, was involved...

Just as Fritz reaches the end of what he has written so far, Dr Kalmenius himself enters the tavern. Everyone but Karl leaves in fear. Dr Kalmenius shows him Sir Ironside, a metal knight that he has made. Karl can solve his problem by placing this in the clock. But the knight is an unusual machine. Whenever someone says 'devil', it relentlessly pursues the speaker with its sword. It stops only when a particular bar of music is sung.

Later, Gretl, the innkeeper's daughter, sits alone by the fire and muses over Fritz's story, unaware of the knight in the corner. She says the word *devil* and inadvertently activates the knight. Inexorably, the razor-sharp sword moves towards her...

Part Two gives a fuller version of Fritz's Story. It explains that the son of Otto and Princess Mariposa was in fact a clockwork figure made by Dr Kalmenius. Young Prince Florian will only become human if he is given a human heart; but 'the heart that is given must also be kept'. Prince Otto gave his heart for his son, but its power lasted only five years. By the time he was ten, Florian was rusting up like an old clockwork toy. A groom takes Florian hunting, then abandons him. Florian arrives at a little town as the clock strikes midnight. He approaches the inn, and as he opens the door he starts to sing his one remaining song...

Part Three brings the two stories together. Florian's song comes just in time to save Gretl from Sir Ironsoul. Gretl recognizes him as the prince in Fritz's Story. The only way he can be saved is if Fritz completes his story. Gretl sets off to find Fritz. Karl returns and sees Florian – a much better metal figure than Sir Ironsoul. He puts Florian in the clocktower, planning to use the knight to make himself rich.

Fritz is packing his bags, terrified by the events that his story has set off. Gretl cannot persuade him to finish it. She heads back towards the inn. Meanwhile, Karl returns to the inn for Sir Ironsoul. Surprised by the cat, he inadvertently sets off the knight – and cannot save himself. Gretl finds Karl dead and realizes what has happened to Florian. She climbs the clocktower; unable to free the Prince, she stays to keep him warm.

In the morning, Karl's body is found. Gretl is missing. Everyone gathers for the appearance of the new clock figure. At the stroke of ten, two new figures emerge: Gretl and Florian. Her love has transformed him from clockwork to human, and they both live happily ever after.

MANAGING THE READING OF *CLOCKWORK*

The Scholastic *Read and Respond* books aim to structure and support children's reading of books in order to improve the quality of their understanding and response. Reflective reading gives children the opportunity to delve deeper into a narrative and its meaning, learning how to read between the lines and developing a personal response. *Clockwork* is exactly the kind of book that repays this level of study. Its complex structure and interlocking narratives can be revealed by close reading and reflection.

The first three **Ways in** activities are designed to be carried out before the children begin to read the book. They should then read the book in seven sections. The first section, the Preface, is supported by a **Ways in** activity. The other six sections are covered by **Making sense** activities. This approach helps the children to look closely at the unfolding story in all its complexity, using their developing knowledge of the story and its characters to make predictions, anticipate events and understand fully how all the parts connect together. The six sections are: Part One to the start of Fritz's story; Fritz's story; from Dr Kalmenius's entry to the end of Part One; Part Two; Part Three to the bottom of page 83; from there to the end.

The **Developing ideas** activities prompt the children to re-read and reflect on the book. They focus on specific episodes in order to explore the key events, themes, characters, story structure and use of language.

The **Evaluation** activities are designed to help the children sum up their reading of the book and their response to it. These activities focus on the book as a whole, making the children put the pieces back together after their close study of various episodes.

CLASSROOM MANAGEMENT

Reading *Clockwork* and working on it can be fitted into the structure of the Literacy Hour. For best results, *Clockwork* should be read with the whole class in a series of carefully-planned reading sessions. This approach is manageable with a book of this length, and it can be used both to support the least able readers and to challenge the most able readers in the class. After you have read a section, discuss it with the class and introduce the appropriate activity.

Many of the activities are suitable for group, pair or individual work. The following activities specify working in pairs or small groups: 'Telling Fritz's Story' (p.9), 'The clock strikes ten!' (p.14), 'Word work' (p.15), 'Language investigation: Punctuation (p.16), 'Solving the mystery' (p.22), 'Who tells the story?' (p.24) and 'The Post-It Notes Master Plan' (p.25).

Those activities for which the children will need to refer directly to *Clockwork* are marked with ☐. It is advisable to invest in at least six copies of the book, so that groups and pairs can work independently. If the whole class is working on the book, plan the lesson so that some children can work on activities which do not require close attention to the text while others are using copies of the book.

DIFFERENTIATION

This book provides a range of activities which you can adapt to match the needs and abilities of your class. Most of the activities are designed to be accessible to children in Years 5 and 6 (P6 and P7), and differentiation comes through the level of response.

The activities on pages 6, 14, 16, 17, 19, 22, 24, 25 and 27 may require some teacher support and mediation. Some activities may be more successful if the teacher provides a model for the children to follow. Individual writing tasks may require additional support in the form of writing frames.

The notes on pages 30–32 give guidance on differentiation, and suggest ideas for extension work to challenge more able children.

TIME-SCALE

Reading *Clockwork* does not take very long. It is a highly condensed book in which the stories interconnect and the narrative ticks away at a steady pace. *Clockwork* is accessible to a wide range of reading abilities: it can be read at many levels, and will challenge the most able in any class. If you make the book the focus of the Literacy Hour, you could work on it over at least a two-week period. You may also wish to use time outside the Literacy Hour for the individual extended writing activities.

This time-scale gives the children an intensive and satisfying course of work, without diluting their enjoyment of the book by overloading them. It also teaches them how to look closely at a challenging literary text in order to develop their reading and writing skills.

TEACHING POTENTIAL OF *CLOCKWORK*

The activities are designed to match some of the objectives for Years 5 and 6 in the National Literacy Strategy's Framework for Teaching. The Skills Grid on the inside back cover provides an overview of the reading and writing skills covered by the activities. *Clockwork* also offers learning opportunities in other subject areas:

Science – the idea of time; how clocks work.

Mathematics – ways of measuring time.

Art and design technology – illustration work; thinking about the design of a clock.

RE and PSE – values and beliefs, morality and mortality.

RESOURCES

It would be helpful for the children to have access to a range of dictionaries, including an etymological dictionary. Some basic reference books about punctuation would be useful. A range of reference books about time and clockwork would allow interested children to pursue this theme further.

A collection of traditional stories and supernatural tales, displayed in the classroom and made available for them to browse through and read, would enrich the children's understanding of *Clockwork* by widening their awareness of the genre to which it belongs.

Some information about Philip Pullman is given in 'Authorgraph No.102', *Books for Keeps*, January 1997. Other books by Philip Pullman which the children may wish to read include the following:

The Sally Lockhart quartet – *The Ruby in the Smoke; The Shadow in the North; The Tiger in the Well; The Tin Princess* (all Puffin).

The New Cut Gang novels – *Thunderbolt's Waxworks; The Gas-Fitters' Ball* (both Viking).

Graphic novels – *Count Karlstein; Spring-heeled Jack* (both Yearling)

Young adult novels – *The Broken Bridge; The White Mercedes* (both Pan).

The *His Dark Materials* trilogy – *Northern Lights; The Subtle Knife* (both Scholastic).

WAYS IN
COVER CLUES

Aims: to examine the front and back cover for clues to the book's nature and content; to consider the significance of the two titles.

Teaching points: considering the book's cover and titles before they start reading helps the children to 'tune in' to the genre of the book they are going to read, and enables them to make connections with books they have read before. This supports their reading of the book.

Extension: look at a range of book covers and broaden the discussion by asking questions about book covers in general. *How much do they influence the reader's choice of book? How much do they tell the reader about a book? Is that information reliable?*

WHAT KIND OF STORY IS IT?

Aim: to consider the idea of genre by looking at the elements that make up traditional stories, in order to understand that there are certain conventions which frame and structure stories.

Teaching points: the children's knowledge of fairy stories and supernatural tales should be drawn out in discussion, helping to prompt their responses in the activity.

Extension: look at a range of traditional stories, compare story openings and endings, heroes and villains and their characteristics, settings and themes.

CLOCKWORK: A PREFACE

Aims: to think about the purpose of a preface; to read it closely for clues to what may follow.

Teaching points: the children may need support in discussing these points. It is important that they understand the connections being drawn between time and life and death, and between clockwork and stories.

Extension: children could research clockwork machines and time measurement, using reference books or suitable apparatus.

MAKING SENSE
SETTING THE SCENE

Aim: to summarize what they have read so far by selecting the key features and putting the information into another format.

Teaching points: the children need to be reassured that it is not the artistic quality of their sketches that is important here, but providing the right information (in sketches and words) to help an illustrator picture the scene. The illustrations could include Fritz and Karl, or just set the scene.

Extension: children who have a talent for art, or an interest in it, could draw fully detailed illustrations for display in the classroom.

TELLING FRITZ'S STORY

Aims: to summarize the key points of a story; to think about the skills involved in storytelling; to develop oral and language skills through retelling a story.

Teaching points: emphasize that the children should not try to memorize and reproduce the story as it is written. They can use their own words, as long as they stick to the main points and do not change what happens.

Extension: more confident children could make tape recordings of their versions of Fritz's Story.

DR KALMENIUS

Aims: to consider the character of Dr Kalmenius and review the information given about him by annotating a portrait; to consider who he is; to predict what will happen next.

Teaching points: encourage the children to read the text closely in order to gain **all** the information they can about Dr Kalmenius – not just his physical appearance. Encourage and support discussion about who (or what) he might be: the Devil, a magician, the villain of the story, a mad scientist, and so on.

Extension: provide a suitable reference source for more able children to find out about the legend of Dr Faustus (for example, the *Oxford Study Dictionary*, OUP). They could write a comparison of Dr Faustus and Dr Kalmenius.

THE STORY OF PRINCE FLORIAN

Aims: to summarize the story in Part Two; to compare it with Fritz's version of the story.

Teaching points: make sure that the children 'get the facts straight' before they embark on comparing the two versions. These tell the same story, but observant readers will pick up the differences in viewpoint. Fritz's Story is an oral version, and he starts in the most dramatic place to draw in his listeners. His version is much more flamboyant, with rhetorical questions and exclamations all adding to the effect of reading to an audience.

An interesting plot difference is that Fritz says the Physician 'had an idea' that Dr Kalmenius might have been involved in Florian's illness. But in Part Two, it says that the Physician was 'baffled'. Part Two explains far more than Fritz's story, and brings it up to date. Aside from the obvious similarities of plot, character and setting, the children may notice that both stories are unfinished.

GRETL – AND KARL/KARL – AND GRETL

Aims: to understand the roles of Gretl and Karl in the sequence of events; to appreciate the interlocking structure of the narrative, and how the author creates excitement and suspense.

Teaching points: help the children to complete each of these pages before they use both to see how the events interconnect. It is important for the children to see how Pullman manages the narrative 'swing' during this passage of the book, and how he builds up excitement and a sense of time by using phrases such as 'meanwhile', 'at the same time' and 'and then'.
Extension: children could consider the rights and wrongs of how each character chooses to act. This may lead them to see that there is a moral 'tick' and 'tock', with the good actions counteracting the bad.

THE CLOCK STRIKES TEN!
Aims: to bring the final dramatic episode to life by acting it out; to write an account of the scene informed by this experience.
Teaching points: this is a teacher-led activity. Read the instructions with the children and help them to choose the figures they are going to be. Allow them time to practise their movements. Emphasize that this activity is not about performance or 'acting': it is about using drama to explore what is happening in the story by experiencing the events in role.

When the children are ready, ask them to get into position. Introduce the drama by reading aloud, from 'Nothing was right that morning...' to 'The hour began to strike.' Freeze the drama at the point when the crowd reacts to Gretl and Florian on the ledge. Try to organize the writing in role immediately after the drama.

DEVELOPING IDEAS
WORD WORK
Aims: to learn about suffixes; to develop vocabulary; to spell some unusual words.
Teaching points: more explicit teaching about suffixes may be necessary as a preparation for this activity. It would be helpful to model the process of inventing words. Some discussion of relevant medical terms (such as *claustrophobia* and *laryngitis*) would also be helpful.
Extension: children could do more work on suffixes, prefixes and the structure of words (as outlined in the National Literacy Strategy *Framework for Teaching*).

LANGUAGE INVESTIGATION: PUNCTUATION
Aim: to develop understanding of different punctuation marks by investigating their use in a piece of writing.
Teaching points: Marking up the paragraphs could be a whole-class activity, with the page copied onto an OHT. The focus of this activity is on investigation, working out why and how the punctuation is used. Explicit teaching can follow with the writing of rules. A reference

book about punctuation would be useful for the children. Eight different punctuation marks are used in the passage: commas; full stops; capital letters (to start sentences, and to start proper names); semi-colons; apostrophes (before 's', to indicate possession); a hyphen; brackets; paragraph indents.

When the children have filled in the table, the rest of the activity should be carried out orally (through teacher-led discussion).
Extension: children could produce a new piece of writing using all these punctuation marks.

FINISHING FRITZ'S STORY
Aims: to develop story writing skills by producing a piece of extended writing with a clear focus (the ending); to use a word processor to redraft, edit and proof-read.
Teaching points: remind the children what kind of story this is and what conventions they are working within – that the story has a happy ending, that the villain comes to a bad end, and so on. Encourage them to retell the story in their own words – or rather, the words that Fritz might use. They can embellish the story, but they must keep to the events in the book. Some children may need more support in planning their work, and a writing frame may be needed for some.
Extension: pairs of children could read their endings to each other. The word-processed story endings could be illustrated using clip art, drawings made using a graphics package or scanned versions of children's line drawings.

WORD PICTURES
Aim: to write a detailed description of a scene, using the writer's style as a model.
Teaching points: help the children to appreciate the descriptive techniques that Philip Pullman uses. He appeals directly to the senses, evoking the smells, textures, sounds and sights that his characters experience. Children who are having difficulty in finding ideas for the writing task could re-read and discuss the scene on pages 83–85.
Extension: children's descriptions could be word-processed, illustrated and displayed.

MYSTERY, PUZZLE OR WISH
Aim: to consider the plot conventions in traditional stories, and how these conventions are used in *Clockwork* to develop the plot.
Teaching points: this activity should help the children to understand what is going on as the stories unfold and intertwine. It isolates specific magical elements, suggesting that they are the mechanisms which drive the story. Discussion would help to reinforce this understanding.

Make it clear to the children that the link between each character and a plot element may depend on who said what **or** on who is being talked about. The links can be 'explained' as plot devices, as clockwork mechanisms or as magic. For example, the link between Fritz and his own statement 'If I come up with something good, the devil can have my soul!' could be 'explained' as a bargain that sets the later events in motion. The children should explore the nature of the links orally (through teacher-led discussion) before writing down their ideas.
Extension: children could look at other fairy tales or weird stories and identify the mysteries, puzzles and wishes which drive their plots.

SOLVING THE MYSTERY
Aims: to develop a deeper understanding of the story by discussing its underlying themes.
Teaching points: this could be done as a whole-class activity or in small groups, but the children will need support in teasing out the answers. They should be encouraged to explore the issues, and not to worry about finding 'the right answer' to each question. They should feel that their opinions are valid, and they should be encouraged to support their views with reference to the text.

Note that Dr Kalmenius can be seen as the Devil or a demon, since he exchanges power for souls and grants wishes without explaining the consequences. He is also like Dr Faustus, a scholar who uses science and magic to gain power. Fritz's declaration 'If I come up with something good, the devil can have my soul!' suggests that he is responsible for what has happened. He knows what he has unleashed.

NAMES ARE IMPORTANT
Aim: to consider the names of characters and what they might suggest to readers about the characters and the story.
Teaching points: children may need some modelling to understand this task. Some of the names could be discussed as a whole-class activity, with the teacher scribing appropriate comments. Note that *Mariposa* combines a common name (*Mary*) with the word *poser*, suggesting someone overly concerned with her appearance and image; *Gretl* links with some traditional fairy stories, such as 'Hansel and Gretl'; *Herr Ringelmann* suggests an association with the clock and its chimes; and *Putzi* (the cat) sounds like a German version of 'Pussy'!

WHO TELLS THE STORY?
Aims: to understand the structure of the story as being 'a story within a story'; to explore the role of narrator.

Teaching points: a general discussion of story structures and narrators before this activity would help to support all the children. The first task could be done as a whole-class activity.

EVALUATION
THE POST-IT NOTES MASTER PLAN
Aims: to summarize and sequence the key events of the story; to learn a technique for planning a story.
Teaching points: this could be done as a whole-class activity, using actual Post-It Notes and a large sheet of paper. If the activity is carried out by small groups, they should be mixed-ability in order to support all the children. Emphasize that the children could use this planning technique for their own stories in future. This activity and the two which follow are all relevant to evaluation: the progression from drawing together the overall structure to forming a critical response will help the children to judge the book as a whole.
Extension: children could consider alternative ways of arranging the scenes.

'LIKE CLOCKWORK'
Aims: to summarize the story by representing it in a diagram; to highlight the interconnected structure of the story; to emphasize the link between clockwork and stories.
Teaching points: this activity will help the children to pull the key events and characters together, placing emphasis on the structure of the whole book. Making the clock diagram gives scope for the children's creative ingenuity.
Extension: this activity could be developed to involve the whole class in making a huge clock depicting the events and characters.

REVIEWING *CLOCKWORK*
Aims: to consider some readers' opinions about *Clockwork*; to form a personal view and express it in writing, keeping to a specific format.
Teaching points: the first part of page 27 could be done as a whole-class activity to promote discussion. The quotes are like advertising slogans and use lots of adjectives, some of them quite unusual. Discuss the meaning of the adjectives *Gothic*, *authentic* and *philosophical*, encouraging the children to use dictionaries where appropriate. The *Oxford Study Dictionary* (OUP) has a definition for 'Gothic' which includes Gothic literature.

In the second part of the activity, the children should be encouraged to express their own opinions. Help them to understand the written style of a review.
Extension: children could write a full-length review of *Clockwork* for a children's magazine.